SPECIAL **People** EDITION

DOWNTON ABBEY

ALL ABOUT THE BELOVED SERIES & FILMS

DOWNSTAIRS AT DOWNTON
Domestic staffers assembled in the servants' hall during season 3. Seated, from left: Phyllis Logan, Rob James-Collier, Jim Carter, Siobhan Finneran, Brendan Coyle and Joanne Froggatt; standing, Kevin Doyle, Ed Speleers, Matt Milne, Lesley Nicol, Cara Theobold and Sophie McShera.

CONTENTS

THE MAGIC OF *DOWNTON*

HOW A BUNCH OF POSH BRITS
AND THEIR SERVANTS
WON AMERICA'S HEART

It was, to be sure, an unlikely megahit. When *Downton Abbey* first graced U.S. public television screens more than a decade ago, the *Masterpiece* series seemed tailored for the kind of Anglophilic niche audience that thrills to adaptations of Jane Austen and E. M. Forster (not that there's anything wrong with that). Executive producer Gareth Neame and creator-writer Julian Fellowes offered up a post-Edwardian England populated by nobles—the Earl and Countess of Grantham, their daughters and his formidable mother; along with their butler, housekeeper, maids, footmen, cooks, et al. It all seemed genteelly out of step while Americans binged on sociopathic antiheroes, rampaging zombies and reality stars. But *Downton Abbey* became, in 21st-century parlance, a thing. The interwoven narratives, enacted by a spot-on cast, weren't period pieces but timelessly relatable stories of love, loss, family, folly, social class and sexuality. Fans couldn't wait for January, when the weekly series resumed its roughly two-month annual run. After the sixth and final season came a hit 2019 feature film and now *Downton Abbey: A New Era*. The secret, Fellowes suggests, is that audiences simply like his characters and enjoy spending time with them. "I wanted viewers to wish these people well, wish them luck in their struggle," he says. "They all want to do their best, and I think that's the appeal of the show."

MIGHTY CARSON
Jim Carter as Downton Abbey's head butler Mr. Carson, a traditionalist who runs the downstairs staff with exacting discipline but essential humanity.

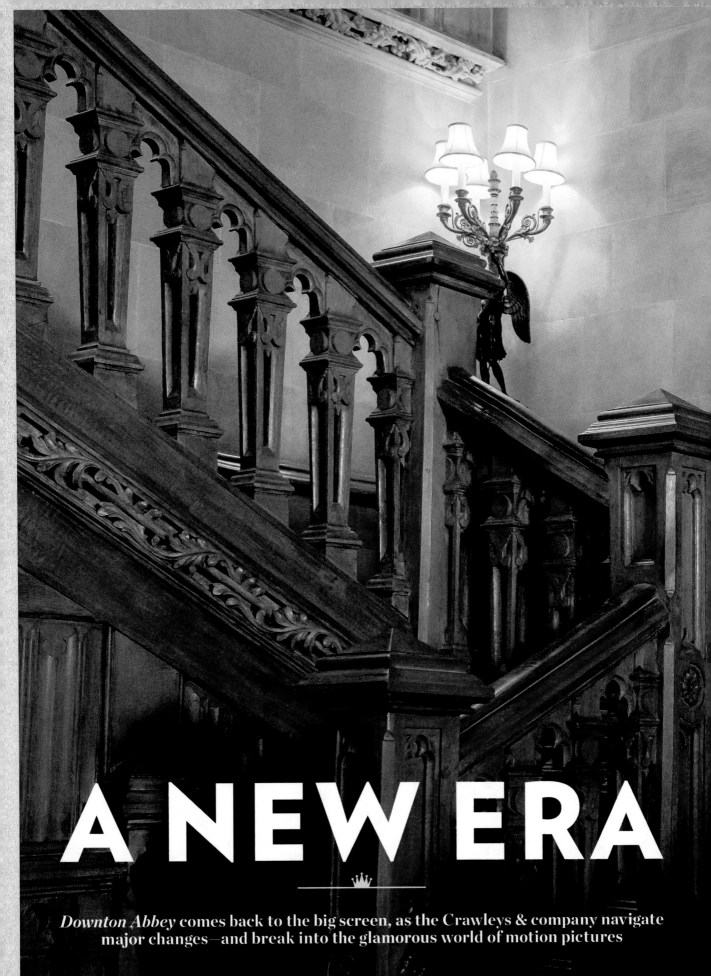

A NEW ERA

Downton Abbey comes back to the big screen, as the Crawleys & company navigate major changes—and break into the glamorous world of motion pictures

THE ARISTOCRATS
Hugh Bonneville as
Robert Crawley, Earl
of Grantham, and
Michelle Dockery as
his oldest daughter,
Lady Mary Talbot.

MOTHER MARY
Lady Mary Talbot (Michelle Dockery) holding daughter Caroline, joined by her aunt Lady Rosamund Painswick (Samantha Bond, left) and Maud, Dowager Baroness Bagshaw (Imelda Staunton).

DOWNTON GOES HOLLYWOOD

INSIDE THE SECOND FILM OF THE FRANCHISE—FEATURING A MOVIE WITHIN A MOVIE

FOR SIX SEASONS, *DOWNTON ABBEY* enchanted television audiences with its addicting narratives and richly compelling characters. Inside a grand Yorkshire castle, the aristocratic Crawleys and their domestic servants played out personal dramas—love and death, triumph and scandal—amid tumultuous world events that unfolded from 1912 through the Roaring Twenties.

Creator-writer Julian Fellowes's masterpiece vaulted onto the big screen with a wildly successful 2019 feature film—fans couldn't wait for the sequel, which finally arrived in the spring of 2022. In *Downton Abbey: A New Era,* the Crawleys are looking to shore up their flagging finances—and so they rent out their home to a silent-movie production company to make a picture. For the duration of the shoot, most of the family—including the Earl and Countess of Grantham (Hugh Bonneville and Elizabeth McGovern) and Lady Edith (Laura Carmichael) head for a villa in the South of France, which Dowager Countess Violet (Maggie Smith) had inherited from a suitor she'd known before meeting her late husband. Meanwhile Violet, her granddaughter Lady Mary (Michelle Dockery) and most of the domestic staff stay on to watch over the proceedings.

The new film brings several new faces, including Hugh Dancy, Dominic West, Nathalie Baye and Laura Haddock. For Haddock, who plays glamorous movie star Myrna Dalgleish, working on location at the real-life Downton—17th-century Highclere Castle (see page 88), home of the earls of Carnarvon—brought out her inner fangirl. "Highclere is really…oh, it's really weighty," she says. "I mean, this is at risk of sounding like a looney, but there were times when I would walk from base camp across to the house and have the theme tune playing in my head. And I was like, 'Okay, Laura, chill out. You're an actress. Go and do your job.' But yeah, it is funny. Something does happen to you there. It is like part of the English heritage now."

DEEP THOUGHTS
Left: Though better known for her witty repartee, the dowager countess (Maggie Smith) has serious matters on her mind in *A New Era*.

STARSTRUCK
Right: Anna Bates (Joanne Froggatt with Brendan Coyle as husband John) shows a movie mag featuring star Myrna Dalgleish (Laura Haddock) to Daisy (Sophie McShera). In the background is footman Andy Parker, played by Michael Fox.

EYE TO EYE
Below: Downton butler Thomas Barrow (Rob James-Collier) has some face time with Guy Dexter, the movie within a movie's leading man, portrayed by Dominic West.

BON VOYAGE
Cora and daughter Lady Edith (Laura Carmichael) sail for the Côte d'Azur. "Oh my God, it literally wasn't work," McGovern says of shooting in the South of France.

DRAMA QUEEN
Right: Laura Haddock as Myrna Dalgleish, the Hollywood silent-film star, brings the pathos while shooting a scene at Downton Abbey.

ALFRESCO IN FRANCE
Opposite top: "I was the French girl in the middle of all those people, and I was a little shy and anxious," says Nathalie Baye (far left at table), who plays the villa owner. "Very quickly they made it easy for me."

MIXED DOUBLES
Opposite bottom: During their South of France sojourn, the Pelhams and Bransons hit the tennis court. From left: Harry Hadden-Paton, Laura Carmichael, Tuppence Middleton and Allen Leech.

HEART TO HEART
Right: Violet with Isobel Crawley Grey (Penelope Wilton). Once adversaries, they've become close friends and companions over the years.

SILVER SCREEN
Opposite top: Dominic West and Laura Haddock in all their black-and-white glory.

HAT TRICKS
Bottom right: As Mr. Carson, Jim Carter shares a scene with his real-life wife, Imelda Staunton, who portrays Lady Maud Bagshaw. (Center: actor Alex Skarbek.)

BUSS STOP
Below: Haddock's Myrna Dalgleish plants one on Charlie Parker's Albert.

DINNERS FROM HELL
Filming meals was grueling for the cast. "They are endless, those scenes," says Penelope Wilton (at head of table). "The camera moves slowly around the table as it becomes hotter and comes back to more dilapidated food each time."

BEHIND THE SCENES

SPLIT BETWEEN BRITAIN AND FRANCE AMID
A PANDEMIC, THE CAST HAD A BLAST

SOME SERIOUS SIDE EYE
Clearly, the Earl of Grantham (Hugh Bonneville) is not amused. Also seated, from left: Samantha Bond and Maggie Smith.

THEY BETTER BE WARNED, the British are coming!" bellows Jim Carter, as semiretired head butler Mr. Carson, to his wife, Mrs. Hughes (Phyllis Logan), near the beginning of *Downton Abbey: A New Era*. When series creator Julian Fellowes reteamed with director Simon Curtis in the middle of the COVID-19 pandemic to create a second *Downton* film, they ambitiously set out to send about half of the cast to the Côte d'Azur while the other half remained at home, where the Crawleys' grand castle morphs into a movie location. Veteran actors Hugh Dancy, Dominic West and Laura Haddock—who play the movie within the movie's director and stars—were thrilled by the opportunity to join the *Downton* family—and frankly to be working during COVID at all.

"I was at home with the children and really putting on a different hat being mum and teacher full-time," says Haddock. "It was a combination of amazing, getting that consolidated time with them, but also you're just chomping at the bit to get back to work. On March 8, [2021] I walked the children from home across the bridge to their school, and I got a phone call from my agent to say that Simon Curtis wanted to talk to me about the new *Downton* film. I remember having the most genuine feeling of excitement and relief. It felt like I just got out of drama school and it was my first gig. That phone call came at exactly the right time."

For Dancy, who is no stranger to period films and series, COVID protocols made the *New Era* experience a unique one. "I'm very accustomed to seeing actors sitting around in funny costumes on folding chairs waiting to shoot and politely gossiping with each other," he says. "But it's surreal seeing Maggie Smith doing that. Then it's even weirder when people are doing that while wearing masks and so on. It was a

WEDDING VIDEO
Allen Leech (wearing a face shield because of COVID-19 protocols) and Tuppence Middleton view footage of their marriage scene, which opens the new film.

completely surreal environment."

Rob James-Collier, who plays Thomas Barrow, the Crawleys' crafty butler, who is a closeted gay man (homosexuality was illegal in the U.K. at the time), was initially sore that he had to remain in England while his castmates headed for sunnier shores. But he reveals that the action at the Abbey proved far better for his character in the end. "Thomas is always good at blagging himself into certain opportunities, and I thought he might stow away on the ferry or something," he says. "But no, he has to entertain Hollywood royalty." And as it turns out, James-Collier adds with a grin, Thomas had a lot more fun staying back at the Abbey.

James-Collier might be the only cast member who preferred remaining at Downton (actually Highclere Castle, Hampshire home of the Earl of Carnarvon and his wife, Lady Fiona). The actors who made it to France—after being told they might have to shoot in a rainy Scotland instead—were ecstatic over the change of scenery and the opportunity to take over an entire resort and isolate there for a week—COVID again—before shooting could begin.

MEET THE NEW BOSS
Above: Masked crew help set up as Thomas Barrow (Rob James-Collier), who succeeds Mr. Carson as butler, now commands the head of the servants' hall table.

COLLABORATORS
Opposite: "When you get very good actors, they don't just deliver the material, they deliver and improve it," says series creator and writer Julian Fellowes (with Elizabeth McGovern).

GRANDE DAME
Left: "She's so funny, some of the things she comes out with," Michelle Dockery says of Maggie Smith (yes, those are sneakers).

A TRULY NEW ERA
Laura Haddock, who plays movie star Myrna Dalgleish, previously appeared in 2017's *Guardians of the Galaxy Vol. 2* and *Transformers: The Last Knight*.

FAMILY TIES
Downton Abbey: A New Era director Simon Curtis (below, with Michelle Dockery) is married to Elizabeth McGovern. They'll celebrate their 30th anniversary in 2022.

CUTE D'AZUR
Above: Honeymooners Tom (Allen Leech) and bride Lucy (Tuppence Middleton) Branson frolic in the Mediterranean.

WHITE HOUSE
The villa in France that Dowager Countess Violet inherits from an ex-lover—which becomes a getaway for the Crawleys (and much of the cast) during the *Downton* movie shoot.

A TALE OF TWO SETS
The Carsons (Jim Carter and Phyllis Logan) film a scene at London's Ealing Studios. Opposite top: Shooting at Highclere, Haddock took a break with Sophie McShera (left) and Joanne Froggatt (center). "You're not allowed to run about the house like a lunatic," Haddock says of the castle. "It's very strict, and there are ropes everywhere."

"It was fantastic," remembers Allen Leech, whose character Tom Branson kicks off the film with his wedding. "The first day of quarantine, the majority of the cast and crew were having refreshments by the pool, and Imelda Staunton (who plays Crawley relation Dowager Baroness Maud Bagshaw) said, 'Be ready to be professional—you have to work in two weeks!'" The Earl of Grantham himself, Hugh Bonneville, has similarly fond memories: "The reality of filming in 2021 in the middle of a pandemic was complicated, so there was a plan A and a plan Zed. Plan Zed was to take two places in Scotland and stitch them together to look like a French villa, but we got to France at the end by the skin of our teeth. We had a week of being holed up in a hotel with Mr. Carson (Jim Carter, Staunton's real-life husband) trying not to get sunburned by the swimming pool."

Laura Carmichael, aka Lady Edith, was able to summon a certain amount of sympathy for her landlocked costars. "We had a really fun time, especially with the crew; it was a real gift," she says. "I feel for the cast that didn't have that story line, because we had a wonderful time."

According to Dockery, though, the arrangement did wonders for Lady Mary and Lady Edith's relationship—the acrimonious sibling rivalry between the imperious Mary and her often downtrodden (but ultimately triumphant) younger sister was one of the TV series' running narratives.

"What's lovely in the film is that you see Mary and Edith much more settled and really matured as women, and their relationship has evolved," Dockery says. "There are less jabs between the two of them. Maybe it's because they live apart—that's helpful!"

MOVIE MAGIC
"Julian is so skilled in weaving his different narratives together," says Hugh Dancy (with Dockery), who plays Jack Barber, the movie director. "It has a very classic, almost theatrical kind of Shakespeare quality.

A STELLAR ENSEMBLE

Throughout the series, upstairs and downstairs, a gifted company of actors brings Julian Fellowes's complex characters and compelling story lines to vivid life

ABBEY PLAYERS
From left, standing: Jim Carter, Rob
James-Collier, Raquel Cassidy, Kevin Doyle,
Laura Carmichael, Allen Leech, Hugh
Bonneville, Michelle Dockery, Matt Barber,
Lesley Nicol, Sophie McShera, Phyllis Logan;
seated: Penelope Wilton, Maggie Smith,
Elizabeth McGovern and Lily James.

**A DANCE TO
THE MUSIC OF TIME**
"Growing with somebody
creates such an amazing
opportunity for an actor,"
McGovern says of
her onscreen marriage
to Bonneville.

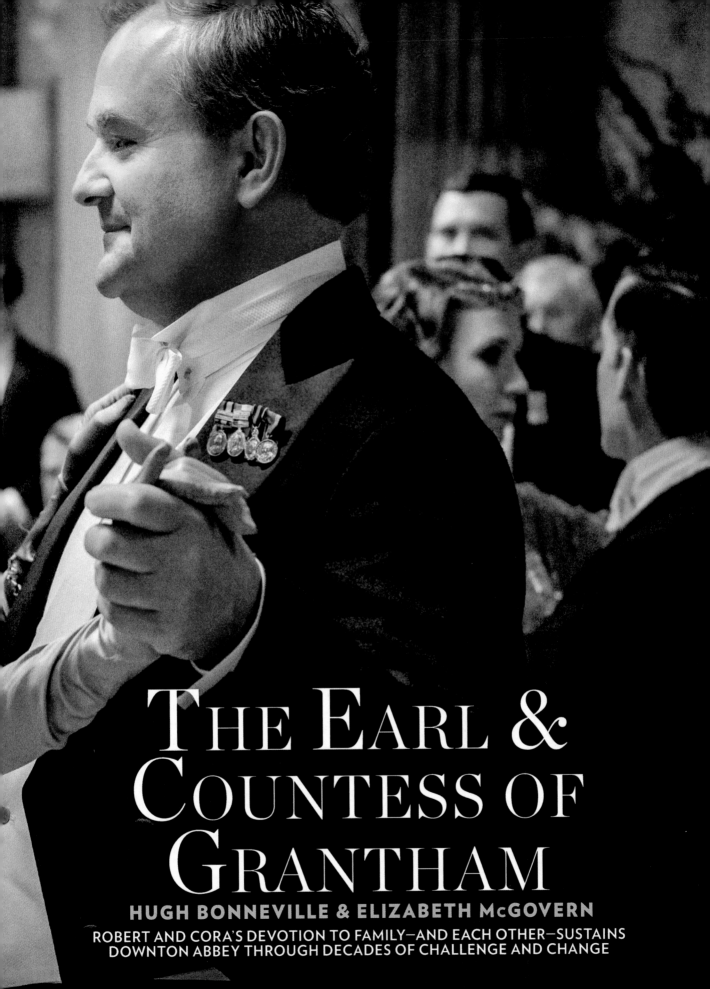

The Earl &
Countess of
Grantham

HUGH BONNEVILLE & ELIZABETH McGOVERN

ROBERT AND CORA'S DEVOTION TO FAMILY—AND EACH OTHER—SUSTAINS
DOWNTON ABBEY THROUGH DECADES OF CHALLENGE AND CHANGE

It may not be an equitable partnership by today's standards, but the marriage of Cora and Robert Crawley is a paradigm of enduring love. Played by Hugh Bonneville and Elizabeth McGovern, the couple have navigated cultural differences— she the Cincinnati-born daughter of a Jewish dry-goods magnate, he a stalwart member of the firmly Anglican British upper class. Together they share the occasional eye roll at the tensions of family life, when even a grand home isn't always big enough to contain the annoyances of drama-queen daughters and problematic mothers-in-law (his mother played by the indomitable Maggie Smith, and hers by Shirley MacLaine, who joined in season 3 as an occasional—and bracingly irreverent—visitor). Over the years Cora and Robert both experience illicit impulses as well as shared griefs, particularly over the death of their youngest child, Sybil. Yet no matter the difficulties, they always wind up in each other's arms at the end of the day.

What do you admire most about Cora and Robert's marriage?
ELIZABETH McGOVERN It was such a wonderful opportunity to see two different people negotiating things over the course of many years.
HUGH BONNEVILLE They faced birth, marriage and death many times—and temptation on both sides. They've been through it all. They've lost a daughter and gone through hardships, some of their own making—mostly Robert's—but there's always a resolution. They're great role models.

Did you find anything less than admirable about your characters?
McGOVERN I certainly felt how frustrating it was for a woman at the time. Cora had no power over her own money—over pretty much anything—and she handles it gracefully. She always put the men first, but I felt frustrated on her behalf.
BONNEVILLE I completely get it. But Robert is the first to acknowledge that the women not only run the place but run rings around him. I mean, it's a wonky system that Cora brings a lot of money to the estate, and I get to play with it and then lose it all to a Canadian railroad.

How do Robert and Cora change over the course of the series?
BONNEVILLE In the first season I really liked Robert's balance of being born a conservative, but he has a liberal outlook on life. As the seasons go on, he seems more like a dinosaur. I said to Julian Fellowes, "He seems to be going down," and he said, "Don't you worry." By the sixth season, I think he's back to a nice balance.

FOR BETTER AND FOR WORSE
"Julian always puts characters to a stress test," said Bonneville (fretting over an ailing Isis with McGovern, top, and with Edith [Laura Carmichael] and grandson George).

" **I REMEMBER THE VERY FIRST READING, WHEN THE ACTORS SAT AROUND AN INCREDIBLY LARGE TABLE... THERE'S A LONG ROAD BETWEEN THAT AND WHAT IT'S BECOME"**
—ELIZABETH McGOVERN ON *DOWNTON ABBEY*

McGOVERN I'm not sure there's very much change in Cora. She's one of the characters people like to depend on. There were times as an actress where I would have loved her to have a struggle to overcome. **Did you have a favorite scene together?**
BONNEVILLE After the death of Sybil...
McGOVERN I completely agree.
BONNEVILLE Their relationship is fractured, and grief affects people at different rates and in different ways. There's a touching scene when Elizabeth confronts me, and she is magnificent in that. She was under a huge amount of pressure, the clock was running out—it was the end of the day—and there was such huge emotion.
McGOVERN What a nice thing to say. The writing was so beautifully delineated about the stages of grief and what it does to people. So much of what you see on TV is fractured relationships, which makes for great drama, but it's so nice to see two people working it out over the years. It's inspiring.

VETERAN TROUPERS
McGovern made her movie debut in 1980's *Ordinary People*. Bonneville played Laertes to Kenneth Branagh's Hamlet with the Royal Shakespeare Company in the early '90s.

LADY MARY TALBOT

MICHELLE DOCKERY

WHETHER HAUGHTY AND NASTY (ESPECIALLY TO EDITH!) OR TENDER AND VULNERABLE, THE OLDEST CRAWLEY GIRL IS A SURVIVOR

AS LADY MARY Talbot (neé Crawley), Michelle Dockery perfects the art of a withering glance, especially when long-suffering sister Lady Edith (Laura Carmichael) is within sight. Mary is also cool under pressure and an adept problem solver, with a remarkable ability to move through tragedies, whether scandalously losing her virginity to one Mr. Pamuk, who dies in the act, or losing her husband, Matthew (Dan Stevens), in a car wreck when she's just given birth. But for all her brisk brilliance, Lady Mary does occasionally show a soft spot; she's devoted to Matthew, charming with second husband Henry (Matthew Goode) and tender with stately butler Mr. Carson (Jim Carter). Says Dockery: "I don't think I'd change anything about Mary." The actress shares why this lady of the manor bows to no one.

KEEP CALM AND CARRY ON
I love her stoicism. I love that she can pick herself up and find the best in whatever she's doing and that she's always got a plan.

GROWING PAINS
Having a man die in her bed makes her grow up fast—she has a secret and has to protect herself and her family. Maybe Mary should have resisted the advances of Mr. Pamuk—she would have had far less trouble knocking at her door—but it makes her who she is. Up to that point Mary was the spoiled oldest child. But she matures with each year, becoming a mother, then losing her husband and her sister.

SIBLING RIVALRY
Sometimes I would be like, "Come on, Mary, be a bit nicer to Edith," but it's because she's not happy. The really challenging times were post-Matthew, when she's vicious. It couldn't get worse than the moment when Mary calls Edith a bitch, and she really has to look in the mirror and realize she's destroying everyone.

THE UPSIDE OF DOWNSTAIRS FRIENDSHIPS
Mary and Carson's relationship is one of my favorite in *Downton Abbey*. Anytime there was a scene between the two, it really excited me, because there are such tender moments. He's like a father figure—he gives her such good advice, and he has her back. And Mary and Anna [her maid, played by Joanne Froggatt] have this wonderful relationship, where they have really helped each other through so much.

SHE WINS IN THE END
I really loved season 6 for Mary, because she's resisting Henry, even though he's so right for her. I love that push and pull and playing the contrary side of her—and also all that anger, because she can't let go. It's rewarding, because of course she finally does and finally finds happiness.

NOT TO BE TRIFLED WITH
"She's a tough cookie," Dockery says of Mary. "She comes from a line of really strong women, and she's inherited that from her grandmother and mother."

LOOKING AHEAD
In 2022 Dockery will star as a sex-crimes prosecutor in the highly anticipated Netflix adaptation of Sarah Vaughan's novel *Anatomy of a Scandal.*

Downton's Mary Men

Lady Mary Crawley's aristocratic reserve masked a passionate nature. Over the course of the series she experienced a scandalous tryst, true love—then tragic loss—and several failed relationships before settling down with second husband Henry Talbot.

HEARTTHROB
The shocking death of husband Matthew (Dan Stevens) "shifted Mary's journey," Dockery says.

ANTHONY, LORD GILLINGHAM
TOM CULLEN
A longtime family friend, "Tony" proposes in season 4. Still grieving Matthew, Mary turns him down.

HENRY TALBOT
MATTHEW GOODE
Dashing, with a scary (given Matthew's death) love for racing cars, he lands Mary and opens an auto business with Branson.

KEMAL PAMUK
THEO JAMES
In season 1 the young Turkish diplomat seduces Mary—then dies of a heart attack in her bed during intercourse.

SIR RICHARD CARLISLE
IAIN GLEN
The ruthless tabloid mogul suppressed the Pamuk affair to protect Lady M., then used it to keep her under his thumb.

EVELYN NAPIER
BRENDAN PATRICKS
Modest and unfailingly decent, he's smitten with Mary. She doesn't reciprocate, but he remains a loyal friend.

CHARLES BLAKE
JULIAN OVENDEN
Inspecting the estate for the government, he clashed with Mary. They bonded in the mud. She cooked him eggs. The end.

CLASS COUPLING
"Who else could we have got together with?" says Carter of their characters. "I can't make friends with the people upstairs. And my status doesn't allow me to make friends with anyone else downstairs except for the housekeeper."

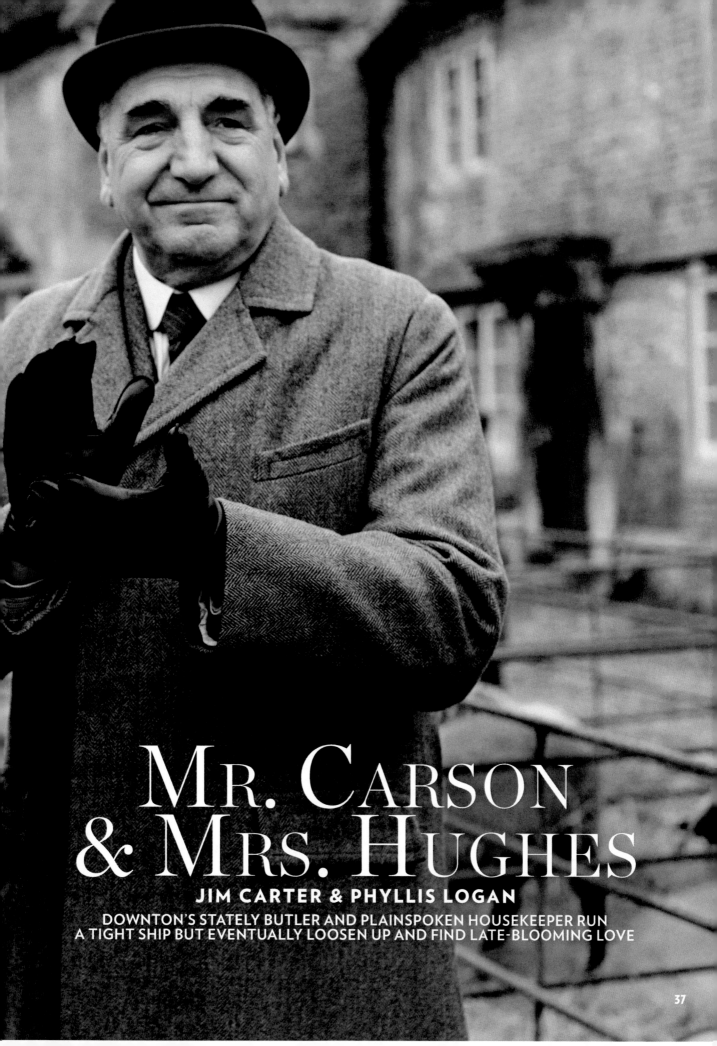

MR. CARSON & MRS. HUGHES

JIM CARTER & PHYLLIS LOGAN

DOWNTON'S STATELY BUTLER AND PLAINSPOKEN HOUSEKEEPER RUN
A TIGHT SHIP BUT EVENTUALLY LOOSEN UP AND FIND LATE-BLOOMING LOVE

Romance on *Downton Abbey* wasn't left to just the youngest members of the Grantham family. By the fourth season, viewers got the relationship they'd hoped for between two of the series' biggest fan favorites: proper but tender head housekeeper Mrs. Hughes (Phyllis Logan) and austerely old-school butler Mr. Carson (Jim Carter). After reading Julian Fellowes's initial scripts, the West End theater veterans leaped at the opportunity to be a part of *Downton,* well before their characters ever dreamed they'd marry and move out of the main house.

How much of Mrs. Hughes and Mr. Carson were mapped out for you when you signed on to the project?

JIM CARTER We were shown [scripts for], I think, three episodes, and on those we had to judge whether to sign on. They wanted to sign options for three [seasons], which is something I'd never done before. But I thought this was a gamble worth taking, because I thought the first three episodes were really strong, and the fact that Maggie Smith was already signed on to it was a good sign. And we also had the history of seeing how [Fellowes-scripted] *Gosford Park* had worked. So we kind of knew that this was going to be a quality piece of work. But in terms of the mapping out of the characters, that wasn't there before.

PHYLLIS LOGAN All we had were the scripts and the characters. The characters were well-drawn, so you knew exactly what your character was like. You didn't necessarily know what fate was going to deal them, but you certainly knew the characters; he drew them very precisely and carefully.

FAN FAVORITES
Traditionally butlers and housekeepers remained single, figuratively "married" to their employers. But viewers "were egging us on to get together," Logan says.

CARTER At the end of season 1, I remember writing an email to Julian Fellowes and Gareth Neame, the head of [production company] Carnival, saying, "You do know that eventually Mr. Carson and Mrs. Hughes are going to have to get married." Well, they did stretch that out for four [seasons] before it happened. But I think that was just down to our—does it sound vain if I say our chemistry? I mean, the way we work together. I think the air of romance wasn't in the script, that just developed. Is that right, Phyllis?

LOGAN Oh, definitely. On a lot of American shows, your trajectory's mapped out, and obviously, come season this, this is going to happen and that's going to happen. There was absolutely none of that at all. I thought it was quite encouraging that the audience should be so invested in this post-middle-age romance that they wanted to see blossom. It was really quite lovely.

Do you have a favorite scene you did together?

LOGAN Oh, there's been lots, haven't there? I mean, it was lovely when you proposed to me.

CARTER Yes. Very rarely did we get to do personal scenes; we were so often in group scenes with the mass of servants. And then when we got those quiet moments in Mrs. Hughes's sitting room with a glass of sherry together and those more personal moments, and you saw behind the pompous butler or the efficient housekeeper. Those were all favorites. But the proposal scene, the paddling scene, was actually my favorite. When we go paddling and holding hands in the sea. That was a favorite.

Do you remember the moment you realized *Downton* had become a global phenomenon?

> " I WAS WALKING IN NEW YORK, NEAR CENTRAL PARK, AND SOMEBODY SAID, 'I RECOGNIZE THOSE EYEBROWS'"
> —JIM CARTER

LETTING THEIR HAIR DOWN
Logan and Carter (at the series wrap party in 2015) are both married to actors who appeared in the *Downton* franchise. Her husband, Kevin McNally, played wealthy, bullying Horace Bryant, whose son impregnated maid Ethel Parks; Carter's wife, Imelda Staunton, is Lady Maud Bagshaw.

LOGAN I got to go to the White House and meet Michelle Obama, in person. She came in; she wanted to meet us all when we were there for one of the 30 Christmas parties they hosted over the season. She came in, bounded up, gave us all a big hug and then regaled us with her wit, wisdom and deep humanity. It was thrilling. I just thought, "I can't believe I'm in the White House and I'm talking to the First Lady." It was just phenomenal.

CARTER I was cycling in Cambodia around the temples of Angkor Wat in my Lycra, what you call Lycra spandex or something, whatever. My cycling gear, which is really a revolting sight, I have to say, purple and sweaty and somewhat exhausted. And a bus full of Chinese tourists pulled up next to us. And one of them went, "Mr. Carson." Now that is just bizarre. It really went everywhere.

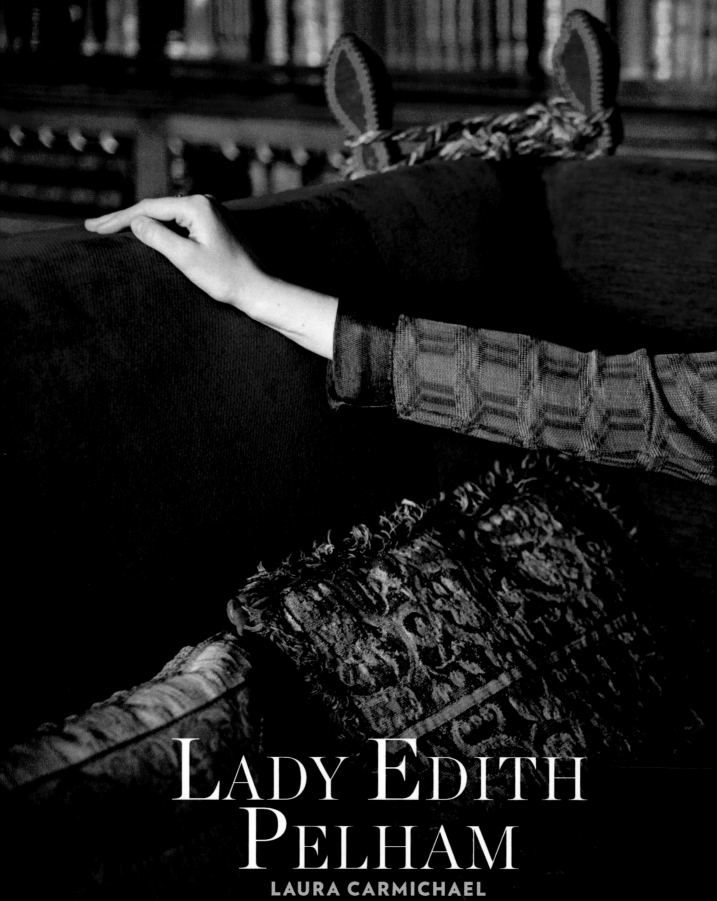

Lady Edith Pelham

LAURA CARMICHAEL

A CLASSIC MIDDLE CHILD, BULLIED BY HER BIG SISTER AND UNLUCKY IN LOVE, SHE FINDS HER VOICE AND TRIUMPHS AT LAST

HEARTBREAK KID
"I always felt for her," Carmichael says of hard-luck Edith. "That means you can enjoy when she's awful and catty because you know where that came from."

COMING INTO HER OWN
A perennial also-ran at Downton, Edith finds her calling—and a whole lot more—as a London magazine publisher.

AS IN ANY GRIPPING drama, most characters in *Downton Abbey* ride a roller coaster of highs and lows. The middle Crawley daughter, however, spends much of her time in an abyss. In the first episode, Edith learns that her cousin Patrick, who is engaged to her older sister Mary, but with whom she is in love, has died in the sinking of the *Titanic*. "She was truly heartbroken," says Carmichael.

Things don't improve any time fast, as Edith is spurned by would-be suitors—and perpetually sniped at by the more glamorous Mary. Finally, in season 3, life takes a turn for the better with the appearance of a doting lover—her editor Michael Gregson. But this is Edith, after all: So of course, Gregson's married, she falls pregnant, and he turns up dead. "I do really love her, but she's forever the drama," Carmichael says of Edith with a laugh. "I can cry really quickly on cue now."

Midway through the series, the actress admits she approached writer-creator Julian Fellowes and asked him to give Edith a break. "It's such a gift for an actor to have meaty story lines, and I feel like I got several," Carmichael says, "But it was such a long burn. I was always nudging him. I would say, 'Please don't kill Gregson.' And he would say, 'I'm going to. But just wait. It's a long payoff, but it's worth the wait.'"

Fellowes did plenty to keep Edith occupied: When marriage clearly isn't in the cards, Edith's determination to escape the confines of Downton leads her to living part-time in London, where she discovers her vocation taking over Gregson's job as a magazine editor. "She finds satisfaction in having something to do," Carmichael says. "I loved her whole world in London. You get this breath of fresh air."

Eventually Edith gains the confidence to reclaim the daughter she gave up for adoption and to acknowledge to her family that she bore a child out of wedlock. "She has more of a backbone, and she becomes an independent woman who has less to lose and isn't afraid to say what she's thinking," Carmichael says.

Still, this is a world in which a love match—or at least a proper match—is the ultimate goal for an aristocratic woman. Carmichael says she kept the faith for Edith, and both the actress and character are finally rewarded with the appearance of Bertie Pelham. When the two meet at the end of season 5, Bertie is a lowly estate agent, but he and Edith are determined to marry, class differences notwithstanding. In a swoonworthy twist, he eventually inherits a most impressive title to bestow on her.

"Julian figured out a way to end the show with this final happy ending: Edith's surprise fairy-tale wedding," Carmichael says. "And while it's really fun playing her happy, I wouldn't change any of it."

REAL-LIFE ROMANCE
Carmichael and *Downton*'s Michael Fox, who plays Andy Parker, went public with their relationship in 2016.

Rocky Road to Love

JILTED, THEN BEREFT, EDITH SEEMED DOOMED TO A LIFE OF LONELINESS—UNTIL SHE WASN'T

DUMPED AT THE ALTAR
Lady E. suffers public humiliation when widower groom Sir Anthony Strallan (Robert Bathurst) bolts at the very last minute.

TRAGIC END OF THE AFFAIR
Married editor/baby daddy Michael Gregson (Charles Edwards) heads to Germany for a divorce and gets murdered by Nazi thugs.

THIRD TIME'S THE CHARM
Edith finally hits the jackpot with estate agent Bertie Pelham (Harry Hadden-Paton), who inherits a title grander than the Granthams'.

DOWNTON STRONG
"I think the viewers really invested in that relationship, which was a real joy for Brendan and myself," Froggatt says of the staunchly supportive Bates and Anna.

John & Anna Bates

BRENDAN COYLE & JOANNE FROGGATT

THE VALIANT VALET AND THE LOYAL LADY'S MAID FORGE A LOVE THAT ENDURES THROUGH HARDSHIP AND CALAMITY—AND ONLY GROWS STRONGER

EVEN DIE-HARD *DOWNTON* fans may forget that the very first character to appear onscreen in the series is dashing, enigmatic John Bates (Brendan Coyle), who is seen taking the train to his first day on the job as the Earl of Grantham's valet. When Bates shows up with a cane and a significant limp, he's met with hostile skepticism from everyone except head housemaid Anna (Joanne Froggatt). Despite an immediate spark between the two, theirs was a relationship that would take time to unspool.

"When I auditioned, Brendan was already cast as Mr. Bates, and they had originally envisaged an older actress playing Anna," remembers Froggatt, who at the time was 30 to Coyle's 48. "They really loved my audition, but because there's an age gap between us, they weren't sure how to make that work." Series creator Julian Fellowes had originally written a fairly short courtship for the couple, but after Froggatt was cast, he changed their evolution slightly. "They decided to…make that relationship between Anna and Bates a bit more of a slow burn, so it starts as a friendship with a shared strong moral code, that they were both incredibly decent human beings with a real respect and love for each other. It made their relationship all the more romantic."

As it turned out, the couple would require a very solid foundation to handle all manner of hardship, including Bates's wrongful arrest and imprisonment for murder in seasons 2 and 3, and Anna's rape in season 4, a story line Froggatt is especially proud of. "It was a huge responsibility and one I took very seriously, and I thought it was brave of *Downton* to tackle that subject matter, and I was really proud that they did," says the actress. "And then moving forward with the way that affected Anna and Bates as a couple, and then

them trying to conceive a child, it has been incredibly moving and incredibly meaningful to tell their story."

When we meet up with the Bateses and their young son in the latest *Downton* film, times are certainly sunnier, a mood Froggatt says more closely resembles her years playing Anna. When asked about her funniest on-set memory, she doesn't hesitate: "Any scene with Brendan Coyle." In fact, the entire downstairs crew keeps things light. "In the servants' hall with 12 of us around the table, and we all have one line each—those are the scenes where I get giggles, because we have a lot of big personalities. Brendan is always making everybody laugh, so is Rob James-Collier, Phyllis Logan, Lesley Nicol, Sophie McShera, Jim Carter, everybody. Numerous times filming the movie, I was in tears with laughter."

A TUBE-TESTED TEAM Yorkshire-born Froggatt and the Dublin-trained Coyle both racked up extensive TV credits before coming to *Downton Abbey*.

SINGLE DAD
Leech with actress Fifi Hart, who played Sybbie,
Tom Branson's child with doomed wife—and youngest Crawley
daughter—Sybil (Jessica Brown Findlay).

TOM BRANSON

ALLEN LEECH

AS THE CRAWLEYS' SOCIALIST CHAUFFEUR TURNED SON-IN-LAW,
HE HELPS KEEP DOWNTON—AND THE AUDIENCE—GROUNDED

ALLEN LEECH joined *Downton Abbey* for the final four episodes of season 1, costarring as Tom Branson, a socialist Irish chauffeur for the Grantham family. As far as Leech knew, that was the beginning and end of his character—until the series was renewed and creator and writer Julian Fellowes determined that Branson was far more useful than simply as a driver.

"Ultimately Branson is a fish out of water," Leech explains, "and Julian said that Tom would be a great character for the audience to latch on to, since he's discovering this world as the audience is doing the same." By season 2, he's also discovered Lady Sybil (Jessica Brown Findlay), and they begin a clandestine romance. "I loved his passion for her and his falling in love with her rebellious, strident attitude," says Leech. "Their love is so pure."

But it can't be sustained at Downton, and the couple abscond to Ireland, where Branson can join the fight to emancipate the country from Britain and Sybil can live without being shunned for marrying the former help. "In a world where so many are brought together for the sake of an estate or marrying for a title," Leech says with admiration, "these two left all of that just to be together."

They're not gone for long: When Branson gets into trouble for joining an uprising, he flees back to Downton, a pregnant Sybil in tow. But there will be no happily ever after: In season 3 Sybil dies as a result of childbirth, leaving her widower bereft—and the actor who played him possibly out of a job.

"I still owe Jessica money, because I lost a bet," Leech says with a laugh. "When she left, I said, 'That's me gone too; I can't see

how I stay on.' But Julian didn't do the easy thing, which is to send him packing, and instead used him to delve into the difficulties of being out of place there. The one person who tied him to the estate is gone, and now he has the responsibility of a child."

While Branson does talk repeatedly about getting out of Downton to recover his independence, and indeed departs briefly for Boston, he eventually embraces his role in the Grantham family, politics notwithstanding. "Tom never gives up on his principles," Leech says. "I love that he does the right thing for himself."

As an Irishman who studied the country's history in school, the actor says, "I had a pure understanding of who this person is and how he would have felt. So much of what he sees is nonsense, but rather than letting it change him, he makes the world he lives in change a bit. He makes Downton a better working estate, and he creates more jobs, bringing some of his socialist attitudes and adopting them."

Branson is less successful when it comes to finding love again after Sybil, despite a flirtation with a local schoolteacher. For that, audiences needed to bide their time until the first movie. "Julian makes you wait and wait," says Leech. "But it's always worth the payoff."

DUBLINER
Leech made his professional debut at 16 in a Dublin production of *A Streetcar Named Desire*. His biggest challenge in *Downton* (below, with Hugh Bonneville and Michelle Dockery)? "Trying to remain true to the character, which began 11 years ago," he says, "and finding the through line, so it's a believable performance."

Daisy Mason & Mrs. Patmore

SOPHIE McSHERA & LESLEY NICOL

THE CRUSTY COOK AND HER YOUNG ASSISTANT CLASHED IN THE KITCHEN BUT ULTIMATELY DEVELOPED A TENDER BOND

S ome of the most delicious moments of *Downton Abbey* happen around the dining room table—and none of those meals would have been possible had it not been for the toiling of the cantankerous cook Mrs. Patmore (Lesley Nicol) and her incorrigible apprentice Daisy (Sophie McShera). Though the two began as sparring partners, their dynamic quickly evolved into a downstairs answer to the mother-daughter dramas unfolding upstairs. By the close of the series, the women remain very tied to the estate that brought them together, but both are also eyeing what their lives might be like residing elsewhere someday.

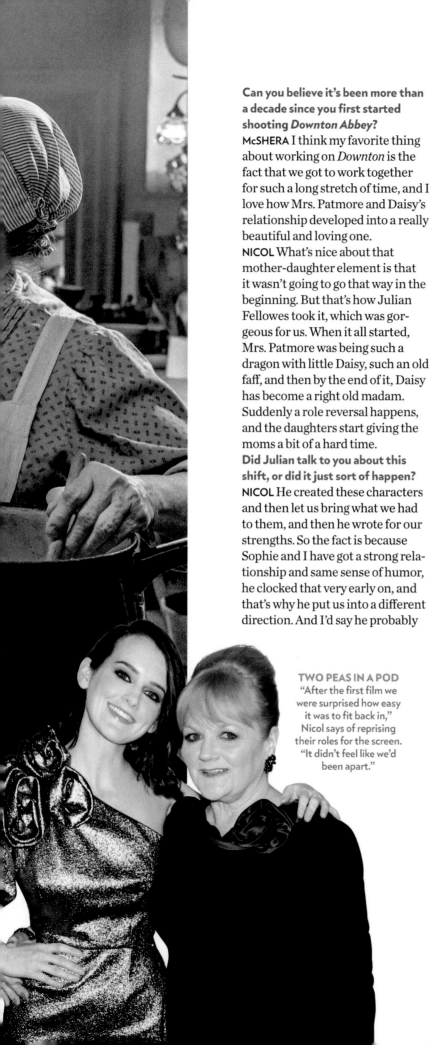

TWO PEAS IN A POD
"After the first film we were surprised how easy it was to fit back in," Nicol says of reprising their roles for the screen. "It didn't feel like we'd been apart."

Can you believe it's been more than a decade since you first started shooting *Downton Abbey***?**

McSHERA I think my favorite thing about working on *Downton* is the fact that we got to work together for such a long stretch of time, and I love how Mrs. Patmore and Daisy's relationship developed into a really beautiful and loving one.

NICOL What's nice about that mother-daughter element is that it wasn't going to go that way in the beginning. But that's how Julian Fellowes took it, which was gorgeous for us. When it all started, Mrs. Patmore was being such a dragon with little Daisy, such an old faff, and then by the end of it, Daisy has become a right old madam. Suddenly a role reversal happens, and the daughters start giving the moms a bit of a hard time.

Did Julian talk to you about this shift, or did it just sort of happen?

NICOL He created these characters and then let us bring what we had to them, and then he wrote for our strengths. So the fact is because Sophie and I have got a strong relationship and same sense of humor, he clocked that very early on, and that's why he put us into a different direction. And I'd say he probably did that for everybody.

McSHERA Yeah, it's kind of exciting to just trust him and read scripts as they come. I remember when we filmed the series, we'd all be getting the scripts and reading them in the car home from set and getting excited about what was coming up. It must've been series 1, and on the way home everyone was going, "You've got a scene with Maggie, you've got a scene with Maggie!" I thought they were treating me like Daisy and winding me up. I was trying to read it really quickly to get to it, and then I did actually have a scene with Maggie Smith, and I was so excited. I remember just feeling so honored. That was the first time I properly met her, and I actually was working with her, and she was amazing.

NICOL I probably have the least to do with Maggie! I was in a scene or two at a distance, but she never spoke to me, and I never spoke to her. But I'll tell you, quietly waiting around for things to happen we'd have a natter, and that would be fabulous, but that's private, and I'm not going to talk about that. But I have always been blown away by the fact that in the credits, my name would go up and then hers is the next on the screen. Sadly my parents aren't alive, but my God, they would have thought that was the best thing ever. I mean, who'd have thought I'd be in the same bloody thing let alone next to her in the credits. I just never, ever took that for granted. It was such a thrill.

When were you struck by *Downton***'s incredible popularity?**

NICOL We had quite a memorable time at the Broadway theater. We'd gone to this musical called *Once,* and we were just walking toward the theater, and we heard a woman literally scream, "Oh my God, it's Mrs. Patmore and Daisy!"

McSHERA It was wild. And then we got to go onstage at the end of the musical and meet the cast. And we were just like, "What the hell, we're in New York!"

THOMAS BARROW

ROB JAMES-COLLIER

SURE, HE'S AN EMBITTERED SCHEMER—BUT WITH AN ANGUISHED
SOUL THAT LENDS HIM DEPTH AND VULNERABILITY

Thomas Barrow is a hard man to love—but actor Rob James-Collier made him irresistible. The infamously underhanded footman began the series as a co-conspirator with not-so-dearly departed lady's maid O'Brien, whose schemes help him ascend to the title of valet and set him on an often ruthless path toward head butler, which he achieves at the end of the first film. Along the way Thomas falls in love, goes to war and narrowly avoids jail time when he's caught in an underground gay club. James-Collier, who was a relative unknown when he landed the part, has nothing but love for Barrow—and somehow we feel just the same.

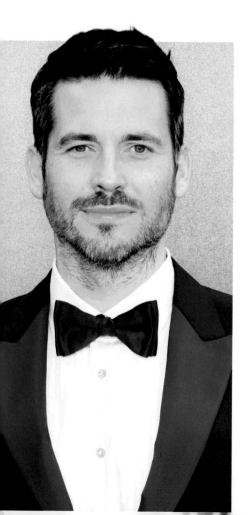

You've been with *Downton* since episode 1. When did you know it was going to be a hit?
I always knew it had a chance because it was written by Julian Fellowes, who got the Oscar for *Gosford Park*. Then at the read-through it really hit home. Dame Maggie Smith is there. I actually sat opposite Maggie, and I was like, "She's here, she's going to do it." That was the moment I kind of thought, "This is going to be a big deal."
Do you remember the first time you were recognized from the show?
I was on the tube, and I saw massive billboards with us all on it everywhere. And I was like, "Wow, they're really going for this." So picture yourself at Oxford Circus tube station when it's busy as hell at rush hour, trying to surreptitiously take a selfie next to yourself on a massive poster.

It's quite hard to do, but I managed. …I sent that to all my mates who I used to play five-a-side soccer with… which I quit to do acting classes, and they told me I was mad.
Do you have a favorite scene?
I like the scene in the first movie where Thomas finally discovered the underground gay club and he's getting that sense of relief and euphoria from being amongst his own. That was a really nice feeling. Just to see how it resonated with the audience when they watched it was quite a proud moment.
What were the unexpected challenges you faced filming *Downton*?
Shaving. I hate shaving. I basically do acting to avoid it, because that's what you have to do in the real world. I had a marketing master's, and they like a groomed man, don't they? So I got into acting, not for a passion of acting or anything like that, just to avoid shaving. Then I find myself working on a flipping period drama for 10 years where every day I have to shave, and then they put these high collars onto the areas that are really sensitive because I never shave. I'm that lazy. I have a real problem shaving, even when I'm getting paid to do it. I'm a pathetic human being. I accept that. But that's my honest answer to your question.

GLAD TO BE OF SERVICE
"My agent rang and said, 'We're doing a *Downton 2*; they'd love you to be in it,'" says James-Collier. "I think my words were, 'Thank bleep.'"

A SLY ONE
In contrast to the dour Barrow, James-Collier is known as an on-set jokester. "I like to riff in the moment," he says, "[with] a kind of surreal, organic, strange humor I find funny, and some people do and some people don't."

MR. MOLESLEY
& MISS BAXTER

KEVIN DOYLE & RAQUEL CASSIDY

HE WAS A DECENT, DIFFIDENT BUTLER WITH A TALENT FOR TEACHING; SHE WAS
A KINDLY MAID WITH A HIDDEN SHAME—AND THEY FOUND EACH OTHER

When Mr. Joseph Molesley (Kevin Doyle) is introduced as Matthew and Isobel Crawley's underutilized butler, he is an earnest, awkward soul eager for approval. For proper approbation, he must wait until season 3 when he moves into the servants' wing at Downton Abbey, but it's not until halfway through yet another cinematic year that he gets a spring in his step. For that, we can thank the appearance of Phyllis Baxter (Raquel Cassidy), a lady's maid whose heart is even larger than the secret she carries. While there will be no consummation by the end of the series, it's safe to say their love for each other is all the appreciation either needs.

Kevin, you came on in the first season. How does Molesley evolve as the years go on?

DOYLE I think at first he is viewed as a figure of suspicion, because he kind of made a move on Anna when Bates's back was turned. But you could feel a gradual change over the years, and he becomes more of a comic relief.

Raquel joined the series halfway through season 4. Did either of you know then that your characters were destined for each other?

CASSIDY I was told there was someone I would have a liaison with, but I didn't know it was Mr. Molesley. Kevin, do you remember when Molesley begins to win her heart?

DOYLE I came to one of your early scenes, when you and Robert [James-Collier, who plays Thomas] were talking about your history. I remember saying to the producers next to me, "This is a great character, and it's going to be really exciting," and they said, "We have plans for you and Baxter," and I said, "Great, great!" [*Laughs*]

How does Mr. Molesley's friendship change Baxter?

CASSIDY She was having such a torturous time of it, first with Thomas, and then risking her future by being honest. That's behind her now, and she has this huge love for Mr. Molesley. While that may or may not be requited, she doesn't ask for a great deal and is therefore happy for what she has.

Do the two of you have a favorite scene together?

CASSIDY My short answer would be every one. But I remember us filming a scene where we were dancing in a group [in the servants' hall]. We were whizzing around the room, being not particularly good

dancers, but Mr. Molesley has quite a bit of abandon in him. And dancing with Kevin is funny, because Kevin is funny. Then Kevin would go off and do some really silly dancing when the camera was off of him, which was an absolute delight.

DOYLE [*Laughs*] Well, thank you! For me, I would say I cherished every scene we had.

CASSIDY Whether it was the comic end of things or the truthful, tough end of things, it's always a blessing to play that with Molesley. That's what you do on- and off-screen, Kevin. It lightens the day.

SIMPATICO SERVANTS
Doyle's humor often broke Cassidy up before a scene. "The first couple of times Kevin made me giggle," she says, "I was like, 'I'm about to go on!'"

ISOBEL CRAWLEY GREY

PENELOPE WILTON

FORTHRIGHT AND SOCIALLY CONSCIOUS, MATTHEW CRAWLEY'S PLAINSPOKEN
MUM PROVES A WORTHY SPARRING PARTNER FOR THE CAUSTIC VIOLET

ISOBEL CRAWLEY is a woman who heeds the call of duty, even after that means uprooting her life in Manchester when her son Matthew is unexpectedly named heir to Downton Abbey. But her sense of righteousness makes this middle-class doctor's widow anything but passive, especially when it comes to pushing back against the aristocrats with whom she is suddenly embroiled.

"I liked her very much. I wouldn't say I loved her at first," Penelope Wilton says of her character, "but I thought she was interesting, because Julian Fellowes used her as a way of looking in on this bubble, which is the world of Downton. At the very beginning she's despised by the aristocrats because she's not wellborn, and she's despised by the servants,

DOWN-TO-EARTH
"She comes to understand the world into which she's been thrust," Wilton, the winner of an Olivier award for her stage work, says of Isobel.

who don't think they should be serving someone of a lower class. "Isobel's the new middle class coming along in 1912, and I was showing a way into that world. I was everywoman."

That's assuming everywoman is willing to take on the imperious Dowager Countess of Grantham, played by Maggie Smith. Isobel is one member of the tribe who is always willing to express her differing opinions, leading to some of the more amusing scenes as the two become fencing opponents and ultimately brilliantly bantering cohorts. "We always had a laugh because our scenes were so spiked, and we enjoyed it," says Wilton. "They aren't cruel, because neither is cruel. It was a game of one-upmanship, and they enjoyed the sparring. It kept them sharp. It kept me sharp."

Gradually Isobel's edges soften as she's welcomed into the family, liberal leanings be damned. "They've accepted her," says Wilton. "She's an integral part of the family and enjoys that."

Nor is she left out of the series' romantic arcs. She deflects the attention of Dr. Clarkson (David Robb), who would seem an ideal match. "I don't think at that time she was thinking about marriage," Wilton explains of their one-sided courtship. "I think she had a good working relationship with him." Love eventually finds her with Lord Merton, aka Richard Grey (Douglas Reith), and when they marry, she ironically becomes a baroness herself, albeit with her moral code strictly intact. "I don't think becoming a Lady interests her that much," Wilton is quick to say, "but what a journey she's had."

While the new Lady Merton may have no regrets, Wilton does have one of her own: "Maggie has the best lines, and mostly I'm on the receiving end of them with my mouth falling apart at her audacity. I would have liked to have got back at Maggie a little more," she says. "I'd like to have had a few more bon mots that squished her. I did say to Julian, 'Please let me win one,' but generally the answer was no. But we always had a good laugh."

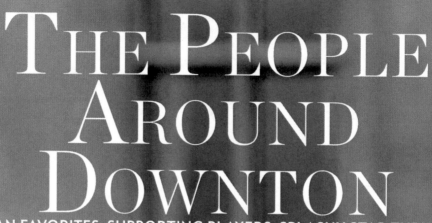

THE PEOPLE AROUND DOWNTON

FAN FAVORITES, SUPPORTING PLAYERS, SPLASHY STAR TURNS: WHETHER THE ROLES WERE LARGE, SMALL OR ALL TOO BRIEF, *DOWNTON'S* GALLERY OF COLORFUL CHARACTERS MADE A LASTING IMPRESSION

ENGLISH ROSE
Lily James as the vivacious Lady Rose MacClare, a distant Crawley cousin who marries banking scion Atticus Aldridge and moves to America.

SHIRLEY SWEEPS IN
As Martha Levinson, Cora's rich and unfiltered American mom, Oscar winner Shirley MacLaine rocks the castle and jousts with Violet.

ETHEL PARKS
AMY NUTTALL
A Downton maid, she gets sacked—and pregnant—after sleeping with a convalescing army officer.

SEPTIMUS SPRATT
JEREMY SWIFT
Violet's dodgy butler is perpetually at odds with her scheming housekeeper Denker (see right).

GLADYS DENKER
SUE JOHNSTON
Violet's scheming housekeeper is perpetually at odds with her dodgy butler Spratt (see left).

SARAH O'BRIEN
SIOBHAN FINNERAN
Before the actress tired of the role, the duplicitous maid plotted constantly with Barrow and caused Cora's miscarriage.

JIMMY KENT
ED SPELEERS
A brash and flirty footman, he competes with Alfred for Ivy—and draws an unwanted kiss from a smitten Barrow.

IVY STUART
CARA THEOBOLD
Succeeds Daisy as kitchen maid; juggles Jimmy and Alfred; leaves for U.S. to work for Cora's brother Harold Levinson.

ALFRED NUGENT
MATT MILNE
O'Brien's nephew is a footman and aspiring chef. Kitchen maid Daisy crushes on him, but he has eyes for Ivy.

SARAH BUNTING
DAISY LEWIS
Progressive—and irritatingly tactless—the schoolteacher carries on a failed flirtation with the widowed Branson.

DR. CLARKSON
DAVID ROBB
The stalwart physician teams with Isobel to turn Downton into a wartime hospital and vainly seeks her love.

HIGH ROLLER
Paul Giamatti (with Poppy Drayton) did a droll turn as Cora's yacht-racing playboy brother Harold Levinson.

THE COOL AUNT
Lady Rosamund Painswick (Samantha Bond) is Robert's outspoken widowed sister from London. Close to Edith, Rosamund offers counsel when her unwed niece falls pregnant.

COURTING CORA
Suave art historian Simon Bricker (Richard E. Grant) breaches Lady G.'s bedroom—in his pj's—sparking a fight with Robert.

Gone Too Soon

Viewers wept when *Downton* whacked these beloved characters (sometimes because the actors wanted out)

MATTHEW CRAWLEY AND LAVINIA SWIRE
DAN STEVENS AND ZOE BOYLE
Matthew's fiancée succumbed to the Spanish flu to clear the field for Mary; when Stevens left to make films, Fellowes canceled him in a car crash.

WILLIAM MASON
THOMAS HOWES
The sweet war-hero footman's deathbed wedding to unrequited love Daisy was a *Downton* tearjerker.

SYBIL CRAWLEY
JESSICA BROWN FINDLAY
Findlay made clear from the start that she'd stay only till season 3; Sybil's death after childbirth devastated fans.

The Dowager Countess of Grantham

DAME MAGGIE SMITH

THE INDOMITABLE VIOLET CRAWLEY REIGNS OVER DOWNTON—AND STEALS THE SHOW—WITH HER REGAL PRESENCE, ACERBIC WIT AND LOVING HEART

"Oh my God, not that I can possibly pass on to you. I mean, literally two things pop into mind, and both of them are brilliant and hysterical and probably libelous."

That's Hugh Dancy recalling his favorite memory of working with Maggie Smith on *Downton Abbey: A New Era*. In addition to being everyone's offscreen MVP, ask any member of the cast to tell you why they were eager to join the franchise, and it always comes back to the wickedly witty Tony-, Emmy- and Oscar-winning actress. In a time when the word "legend" is thrown around all too often, the 87-year-old fully earns that title.

Best known for going toe-to-toe onstage with fellow Brits like Laurence Olivier and Albert Finney and bringing the words of Edward Albee, Peter Shaffer, Neil Simon and Tom Stoppard to life, the West End and Broadway veteran had never starred in a long-running television series when she signed on to *Downton Abbey*. The project reunited her with screenwriter Julian Fellowes, whose 2001 film *Gosford Park* earned Smith her sixth Oscar nomination. (She previously won the award for 1969's *The Prime of Miss Jean Brodie* and 1978's *California Suite*.)

You could say Dame Maggie steals every scene she's in, but even her most high-profile costars gladly hand them over to her. "I was on-set the first day Shirley MacLaine turned up, and the stills photographer was really struggling to get Maggie and Shirley in a photo together, so I grabbed them and said, 'Come on, girls, come here,' and put my arm around them," remembers Jim Carter, who plays Mr. Carson. "Maggie's got a couple of Oscars, and I think she might have reminded Shirley that she had two and Shirley only one. They got on like a house on fire, and to be part of that was magic."

Though it's hard to top her season 1 delivery of *Downton*'s most famous line, "What is a weekend?" Smith has consistently kept her cast members on their toes and audiences in stitches playing the Dowager Countess of Grantham for 12 years, six seasons and two films. It's also a role that has earned Smith three Emmys and more fame than even her appearances in seven Harry Potter films ever did.

"It's ridiculous, I led a perfectly normal life until *Downton Abbey*—I'm not kidding. I'd go to theaters, I'd go to galleries, and things like that on my own, and now I can't," Smith said in 2017. "Life was fine, and nobody knew who the hell I was, and now it's all changed." Still, Smith has never watched an episode of the series, dryly confirming in the same interview, "No, I haven't seen it. It got to a point when it was too late to catch up."

THE MATRIARCH
Michelle Dockery recalls being "terrified" before her first scene with Smith, "but she was so kind. It was like, 'You're playing my grandchild, and it's going to be lovely.' It was so generous and so sweet."

MUST-SEE MOMENTS

AN ALBUM OF SOME OF THE MORE MEMORABLE PLOT POINTS DURING *DOWNTON ABBEY*'S SIX-SEASON RUN ON TV

CRAWLEY & CRAWLEY
After two seasons of jousting, a world war and a global pandemic, Lady Mary and distant cousin Matthew Crawley finally tie the knot.

LOVE AND DEATH—AND THE DOWAGER

Above: In season 1 Violet utters perhaps her most memorable line, "What is a weekend?" Right: In the series' third episode, Lady Mary loses her virginity to dreamy Turkish diplomat Kemal Pamuk (Theo James), who dies suddenly in her bed, forcing Mary, her mother and lady's maid Anna to smuggle the body out of the room. Below: The rapturously romantic moment at the end of season 2 when Matthew, the heir to Downton Abbey, finally kneels down in the snow and asks Mary to be his wife.

CRAWLEYS IN CRISIS
A stormy season 2 for the earl and countess. Above: Cora recovers after suffering a miscarriage. The Granthams' joy over her ladyship's unexpected pregnancy turns to heartbreak when her maid O'Brien (Siobhan Finneran), believing she's about to be sacked, leaves a wet bar of soap beside the bath, causing Cora to fall and lose the baby. Left: Normally above reproach, Robert strays over class lines when he and Jane Moorsum (Clare Calbraith), a war-widowed maid, develop a mutual attraction; it never goes beyond a few surreptitious kisses.

THE ECSTASY AND THE AGONY
Above: The birth of daughter Sybbie in season 3 is an all-too fleeting moment of joy—quickly dashed when Sybil dies of eclampsia seizures. Sybbie, and Tom's anguished grief, earn the former Crawley chauffeur acceptance into the family fold. Below: The third season also features hard-luck Edith's most humiliating blow of all: when fiancé Sir Anthony Strallan (Robert Bathurst), a two-decades-older widower left lame by a war injury, bails on her at the altar. Turns out he did her a favor.

I'LL STAND BY YOU

Valet John Bates and lady's maid Anna Smith's devoted marriage is tested by her rape and his imprisonment on a false murder charge (left, in season 3), among other challenges. Below: After years of working side by side with him—their mutual affection growing ever so gradually—Mrs. Hughes takes Mr. Carson's hand in season 4, as they wade into the surf. It was a heartwarming affirmation of love for fans who feared the pair might wind up like the repressed butler and housekeeper played by Anthony Hopkins and Emma Thompson in *The Remains of the Day*.

A ROSE AND A MARIGOLD

Above: Spirited young relative Lady Rose MacClare raises eyebrows in season 4 when she dances with Black jazz-band leader Jack Ross (Gary Carr). The pair fall in love and talk of matrimony, but Ross ends it, saying he loves Rose too much to put her through the difficulties their marriage would cause. Right: After giving up Marigold, her daughter with murdered lover Michael Gregson, to the Drewes—farmers on the Grantham estate—Edith reunites with the girl for good in season 5.

NEW BEGINNINGS
Left: When scullery maid Daisy weds the gentle, war-injured footman William Mason on his deathbed, she's wracked with guilt because she's not in love with him. But as a widow, she gains a father figure in William's kindly farmer dad, Albert (Paul Copley), who urges Daisy to pursue her dreams of improving her lot in life. Below: Season 6 saw one of *Downton*'s most glorious moments—the marriage of Mr. Carson and Mrs. Hughes. Under pressure to hold the wedding breakfast at Downton, the Scottish housekeeper puts her foot down—and gets the wedding reception of her dreams.

DOWNTON & HISTORY

THE CRAWLEY FAMILY'S UPSTAIRS-DOWNSTAIRS SAGA PLAYS OUT OVER TUMULTUOUS DECADES OF SOCIAL AND POLITICAL CHANGE

1912
TITANIC SINKS
En route from England to New York, the liner hits an iceberg. Among the 1,500 dead: two fictional male heirs to Downton, setting the inheritance plot in motion.

1914
ARCHDUKE ASSASSINATED
Franz Ferdinand, heir to the Austrian throne, is shot to death while being driven through Sarajevo, igniting World War I.

1916
BATTLE OF THE SOMME
The allied offensive in France is one of history's deadliest—and both Matthew and Barrow (below) see action.

1917
THE RUSSIAN REVOLUTION
Bolsheviks topple Tsar Nicholas II; nobles like Violet's ex Prince Kuragin (Rade Sherbedgia, below left) flee the country.

1919
GRAND TRUNK FAILS
The Canadian railway goes bankrupt—losing a fortune for the Crawleys.

1920
WOMEN'S SUFFRAGE
Adult females get to vote in the U.S. (Brits would in stages by 1928.) Edith's letter to a newspaper supporting the cause creates a stir.

1918
SPANISH FLU
The global pandemic causes some 50 million deaths worldwide—including that of Matthew's fiancée, Lavinia Swire (Zoe Boyle).

END OF WORLD WAR I
After four years and 40 million military and civilian casualties, Germany surrenders.

1916
THE HOME FRONT

Like real-life Highclere, Downton was converted into a military hospital during World War I. Here Lady Mary (Michelle Dockery) tends to wounded love Matthew (Dan Stevens).

WARNER BROS. SUPREME TRIUMP
AL JOLSON
"THE **JAZZ SINGER**"

WITH
MAY McAVOY
WARNER OLAND
Cantor Rosenblatt

Based upon the play by Samson Raphaelson as produced on the spoken stage by Lewis Gordon Sam Harris
Scenario by Al Cohn

DIRECTED BY ALAN CROSLAND

A WARNER BROS. PRODUCTION

1922
IRISH FREE STATE

A treaty with Britain ends Ireland's three-year war for independence.

PAS. PASSPORT.
SAORSTÁT ÉIREANN
IRISH FREE STATE

1923
STANLEY BALDWIN

The Conservative P.M. will dominate British politics between the world wars.

1922
RISE OF RADIO

Dismissed as a "fad" by Lord Grantham, the wireless becomes a staple in homes—including Downton.

RADIO NEWS
25 Cents
NOVEMBER
Edited by HUGO GERNSBACK
Over 200 Illustrations

1927
THE JAZZ SINGER

The first talkie heralds the end of silent films just as Hollywood comes to Downton in *A New Era*.

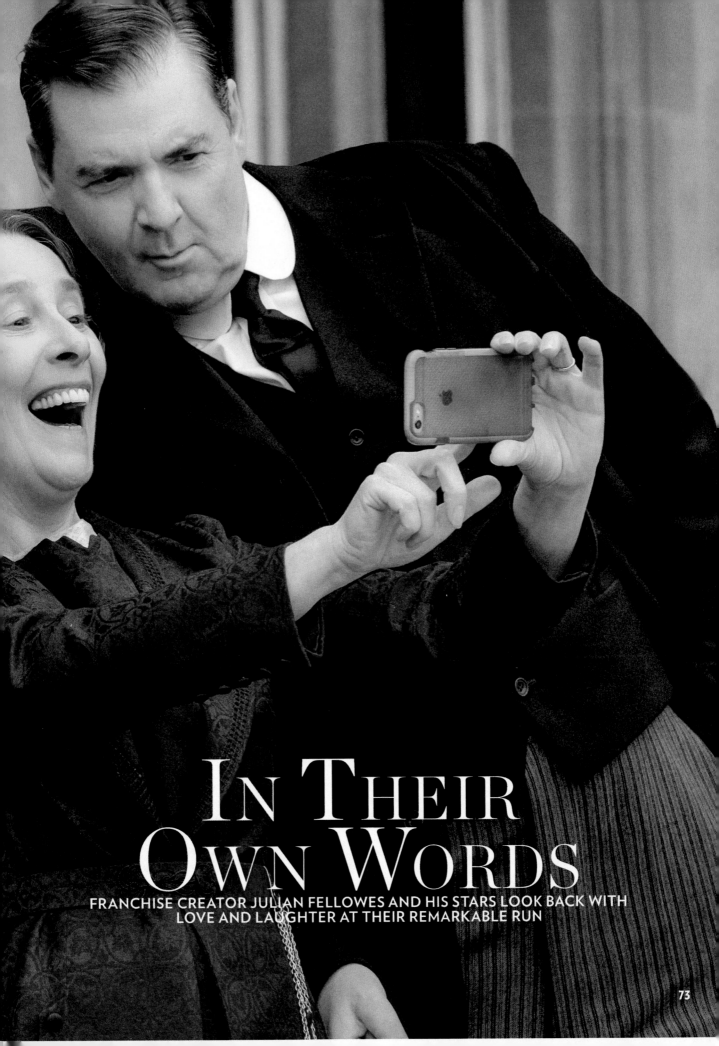

In Their Own Words

FRANCHISE CREATOR JULIAN FELLOWES AND HIS STARS LOOK BACK WITH LOVE AND LAUGHTER AT THEIR REMARKABLE RUN

BRAIN TRUST
It was executive producer
Gareth Neame (left) who
first suggested the
idea of *Downton Abbey* to
Julian Fellowes (with
Michelle Dockery).

Even as *Downton Abbey* offered viewers an escape into the world of the Crawley home, it was a real-life workplace for a sprawling cast and crew. Here the show's creator and cast look back at the things that made them laugh, the scenes that made them cry, lines that made them rap and a dinner scene that made them murderous.

THE ROAD TO *DOWNTON ABBEY*

JULIAN FELLOWES [creator and writer] At the time, now 12 years ago, there was a thinking that period drama was dead—the young weren't interested, it was finished. But we were very fortunate that Peter Fincham, the director of television at ITV, didn't subscribe to this belief. He thought there was an audience if you gave them the right one. When we managed to persuade Maggie [Smith] and Hugh [Bonneville] and that first group of actors to do it, I thought we were going to have a good show. But I had no expectations beyond finding an audience in Britain.

ELIZABETH McGOVERN [Cora Crawley, Countess of Grantham] I don't think anyone knew. I do remember when all the actors sat around this very large table and read the first two episodes; there was a frisson in the air for sure. But there's a long road between that and what it's become.

MICHELLE DOCKERY [Lady Mary Talbot] It was my first big job, so that first year was quite challenging, believing in myself and not letting my confidence drop. The first scene that the three sisters had to do with Maggie Smith, we were all so nervous. We were in the dining room, and she was so kind to us—she made us feel so at ease."

KEVIN DOYLE [Joseph Molesley] I was only contracted for a few episodes. Molesley was there really to introduce Matthew Crawley and his mother to the world of Downton, a world of having servants. Thankfully the producers and Julian decided to keep me along for the ride.

ALLEN LEECH [Tom Branson] I was quite nervous coming into that caliber of actors. But we were only banking on one season. I think for everyone the hope is always that the show will go again, but everyone was wary of it.

HOUSE RULES

HARRY HADDEN-PATON [Herbert Pelham] *Downton* is more detailed than any show I've ever been in, including *The Crown*. [Historical adviser] Alastair Bruce and Julian really care about the period detail, and so there were definitely a few times when I was told to sit differently or take my hands out of my pockets. And every meal, we're being reminded, "You shouldn't hold a fork this way." …As I get older I care less, but there's a code of conduct that you've signed up for. And all the costumes and the strict ethics create so much more drama.

EMOTIONAL RANGE

LEECH The scene where Sybil [Jessica Brown Findlay] passes is one of the best ones, but it was rough. It was shot over three days, and trying to maintain that mental health space was very draining for

all of us. And it was the first time saying goodbye to one of the main characters who had been on this incredible journey with us, so there was lots of emotion."

FELLOWES When I was watching Sybil's death, I was crying, and I said to myself, "You wrote this— what did you think would happen?"

LAURA CARMICHAEL [Lady Edith Pelham] [The show] is so serious, if something goes slightly wrong, it's just hysterical. There are a lot of deep breaths.

DOCKERY If someone fluffs a line, we just lose it. In season 3 they were in Scotland, and Joanne Froggatt [Anna Bates] is getting Mary ready for bed. Mary had been on this horse and trap to go somewhere, and Anna says, "How was the journey?" and Mary says, "I was shaken about in that trap like dice in a cup," and there was something about it that was like a rap,

SYBIL SUCCUMBS
The death of the youngest Crawley daughter (Jessica Brown Findlay) marked one of the strongest episodes, says Allen Leech, who played her husband, "because of the performances. Everyone was so brilliant."

DISHING IT OUT
"I don't think they saw Molesley as being a long-term character," Kevin Doyle (with Maggie Smith) says of Neame and Fellowes. "But in season 3 I became part of the furniture, as it were."

MASTER OF MANNERS

Historical adviser Alastair Bruce is known on the *Downton* set as the Oracle, ensuring filmmakers and actors accurately depict the era. Once the equerry (personal aide) to Prince Edward, Bruce admits being "ruthless" about the subtlest details, whether it's how a lady holds herself or which spoon to use for bouillon. "I've always walked onto a set with innate confidence," he says. "I know my onions, as we say here."

and we started doing it as a song. We were laughing so much we felt like we were in trouble at school, with the director saying, "Concentrate!" while we were falling apart.

HADDEN-PATON I can't be anywhere near Allen Leech or Rob James-Collier [Barrow]. If I'm too close to them, it's trouble. I'm terrible at getting giggles, and I'm like a little boy who is easily manipulated. We filmed in one house that was open to the public, and when you don't have much to do, you have naughty thoughts, and Allen and I decided to hand out the tickets to the visitors. I could not keep it together. But then you risk getting told off by the director, and that's awful.

RAQUEL CASSIDY [Phyllis Baxter] I have a picture I really cherish where we're on a desk, and I'm sitting between Kevin [Doyle] and Brendan [Coyle, who plays John Bates], and I'm laughing my head off because you couldn't have two funnier men.

LEECH If you look closely in many of those dining room scenes, and there's a [funny] look on Carson's face, it's because my shoulders are shaking [from laughter].

TABLE TALK

HUGH BONNEVILLE [Robert Crawley, Earl of Grantham] The dining table scenes are notoriously tricky because they take forever.

McGOVERN They're boring is what he's trying to say. They're so boring. It takes endless hours to do every setup of every person around the table. There was a first assistant director who was one of those people who didn't have a sense of personal space, and by end of day all of us had lost their rag with him. I remember Maggie [Smith], every time he would come toward her, she would stick her cane out. And one day it was so hot we were looking at a piece of salmon on the plate that had already started to turn by 10 a.m.

BONNEVILLE The great skill one

learns is not to eat at all (unless it was a breakfast scene—that cook was fantastic). Because if you eat at one camera angle, you have to eat at all of them. I think over 10 years Maggie ate one pea....To alleviate the boredom, we played a game called Wink, Murder, where everyone takes a piece of paper [with one person drawing the "murder" role]. If that person winks at someone, they die. Sometimes you'd have 20 people playing at a dining room scene, so that was very entertaining.

McGOVERN You'd have to try to be clever enough to kill somebody when they weren't saying a line on-camera, so they wouldn't be seen dying.

LEECH I won many a round of that. The trick is that you don't have to murder everyone quickly; you can do it quite slowly.

A DOG'S LIFE

BONNEVILLE At the beginning of season 2 they said, "Here's Pharaoh," and I said, "That's not

SCHMOOZING BETWEEN SHOTS
Foreground: Penelope Wilton (right) chatted with Shirley MacLaine. "When Shirley came, that was good fun," Wilton says. "She's such a nice woman, and she sang 'If They Could See Me Now' for us."

A GOOD FIT
Hugh Bonneville and Elizabeth McGovern played husband and wife twice before *Downton*: once in a show that never aired and again on the 2008 BBC comedy series *Freezing*.

HAPPY AT LAST
Lady Edith (Laura Carmichael) finally found true love with Bertie Pelham (Harry Hadden-Paton). "I think he's absolutely besotted by her," Hadden-Paton says. "Head over heels."

Pharaoh, that's another dog. This is a bitch, and the other one was a male, and people will notice. But let's keep the Egyptian theme." I suggested the name Isis. As for what happened to the other dog, Pharaoh must have died of boredom. He was a lump and had zero personality.
McGOVERN Poor Hugh. Almost every day he came to the set smelling like dog treats, because he was supposed to have this incredible relationship with the dog. It never worked. The dog would completely ignore him.
LEECH Hugh and I laugh that the dogs were the highest-paid and most disobedient actors on-set. The dog got so many treats, he just gave up and would head off, and we couldn't bribe him anymore.
BONNEVILLE There was one iteration of whatever dog it was that when someone called action, it ran across two counties and just disappeared.
McGOVERN A trained dog.
BONNEVILLE Only trained to run away.
McGOVERN [*Laughing*] Which was what we all wanted to do at a certain point.

THE END OF AN ERA
FELLOWES For the best part of six years, I tried to write episodes that if you were in a hotel room and you tuned in for the first time, you'd still enjoy it. But for the last episode of season 6, I remember consciously thinking, "This is the reward for everyone who has followed it for six years, and I'm not going to worry about other people." But of course, two years later we were hustling them into the theater. I've said goodbye to these characters four times already, and each time I've thought, "The last scene has to work [as] the end."

READY FOR MY CLOSE-UP
The *Downton* dogs were less than cooperative on-set. "They're as bad as actors," says Bonneville. "All they want is free food."

CRAWLEY COUTURE

DRESSING DOWNTON

THE TV SHOW AND FILMS TAKE VIEWERS ON
A DAZZLING SARTORIAL JOURNEY,
FROM THE OPULENT ELEGANCE OF LA BELLE
EPOQUE TO THE ART DECO ELAN OF THE JAZZ AGE

VIOLET IN MAUVE
Maggie Smith's Belle Epoque look as the Dowager Countess (opposite, center) varied little. "Obviously there's the same sensibility, the same sense of style," costume designer Anna Robbins told PBS.

WELL SUITED
Above, from left: Brendan Coyle as John Bates; Hugh Bonneville (Earl of Grantham); Allen Leech (Tom Branson); and Kevin Doyle (Joseph Molesley).

DOWNSTAIRS DRAB
By contrast to the ultrachic Crawley girls, servants such as lady's maid Anna (Joanne Froggatt, right, during the first season, set in 1912) were consigned to dowdy uniformity.

GOOD FORTUNY
Left: For the first film, Robbins reimagined a 1927 Fortuny Delphos gown, adding a V-neck, she told *The New York Times*, to make it "more dynamic, edgier and a bit cooler."

BANGLES & BEADS
Opposite: Season 5, which is set in 1924, saw Lady Mary draped in a beaded necklace and similar headwear.

MADE IN SHADES
Below: In season 6, Lady Mary donned sunglasses to watch future hubby Henry Talbot (Matthew Goode) in an auto race—which ends badly for Henry's pal Charlie.

INSIDE HIGHCLERE CASTLE

THE REAL-LIFE DOWNTON ABBEY HAS ROOTS IN THE EARLIEST DAYS OF
BRITAIN—AND A LINK TO THE DISCOVERY OF KING TUT'S TOMB

HOME AND CASTLE
Opposite: George Herbert, 8th Earl of Carnarvon, and his wife, Lady Fiona, the Countess of Carnarvon, outside Highclere Castle. His family has occupied Highclere since the 17th century. The estate dates to 749; the current house was built in 1679 and underwent an elaborate renovation in the 1840s. This page: the Great Hall.

QUIET, PLEASE
Highclere's Library holds some 6,000 volumes, organized by the Dewey decimal system. The 19th-century room was inspired by London's Reform Club.

DINNER IS SERVED
1. The Dining Room is lined primarily with 17th-century paintings, notably (left) an equestrian portrait of King Charles I by Anthony van Dyck.
2. Mr. Carson (Jim Carter) attends Lady Mary (Michelle Dockery).

LIFE (AND MUMMIES!) VERSUS ART
Lady Carnarvon (with her late yellow
Lab Percy) in the Sitting Room, scene of
many *Downton* moments. Lord
Carnarvon in Highclere's Egyptian
Exhibition (above)—the 5th Earl
(1866-1923) was chief financial backer of
Howard Carter's expedition to find King
Tutankhamun's tomb; his death from a
mosquito bite has been attributed to the
legendary King Tut "curse." Filming in
the Sitting Room (below).

DISH NETWORK
Mrs. Patmore (Lesley Nicol) rules the kitchen (left)—which, unlike the dining room, isn't at Highclere, but on a soundstage at London's storied Ealing Studios.

SPECIALTIES OF THE HOUSE

FOOD, GLORIOUS FOOD: OVER THE YEARS DOWNTON'S STAFF HAS SERVED UP SOME SCENE-STEALING CUISINE

Much of the action in Downton Abbey involves eating and drinking—Mrs. Patmore and Daisy slaving over the stove, footmen serving the Crawleys and guests sumptuous candlelight dinners and elegant teas, Mr. Carson presiding over a long communal table in the servants' hall. Indeed, food is an unbilled character in the franchise—enough to have inspired *The Official Downton Abbey Cookbook*, by Annie Gray, showcasing more than 100 dishes: Upstairs you might sample oysters au gratin, cucumber soup, quail and watercress or raspberry meringues (see page 94); downstairs, toad-in-the-hole

(sausages in Yorkshire pudding batter), steak and kidney pudding or gingerbread cake. During the series it fell to food stylist-chef Lisa Heathcote to prepare each dish in her professional kitchen, then drive it to the set. Of course, little of it was actually eaten—but when it was, historian and etiquette consultant Alastair Bruce was at the ready, offering guidance "There are a number of younger people who eat their way through their cereal without closing their lips," he says. "You can't trust [them] to eat in the form of the 1920s. I'm very conscious to correct people on how to hold a knife and fork and not use the fork without the knife. Food comes in and out on the left and drinks on the right, and footmen leave spare space and—it's a ballet really."

Raspberry Meringues

Meringue with fruit is one of *Downton's* go-to desserts, appearing twice in the first two seasons (including when Mrs. Patmore boldly refuses to change her menu after the Crawleys request an apple charlotte). This one, adapted from *The Official Downton Abbey Cookbook* by food historian Annie Gray, is served with a fool (a mix of cooked fruit and cream).

FOR THE MERINGUE

- 2 egg whites
- 1 teaspoon fresh lemon juice
- ½ cup plus 1 tablespoon (115g) superfine sugar

FOR THE FOOL

- ½ lb. (225g) raspberries plus more for decorating
- ½ cup plus 2 tablespoons (150ml) heavy cream
- ¼ cup (55g) superfine sugar
  Confectioners' sugar, if needed

1. To make the meringue, preheat the oven to 200° (95°C). Line a sheet pan with parchment paper.
2. Using a whisk or a handheld mixer on medium speed, beat together the egg whites and lemon juice in a bowl until soft peaks form, increasing the mixer speed to medium high once the whites are foamy and begin to thicken. Beating constantly, add the superfine sugar, a little at a time, and beat until stiff peaks form. Transfer the mixture to a piping bag fitted with a large star tip. Pipe 6 meringue nests, each 2-3 inches (5-7.5 cm) in diameter—first outlining them, then filling the centres and finally building up the sides—and some small stars for garnish on the prepared pan.
3. Bake the meringues for 2-2½ hours. They should be crisp to the touch and lift off the parchment easily. Let cool completely.
4. To make the fool, puree the raspberries in a food processor or blender, then pass the puree through a fine-mesh sieve to remove the seeds, or use a food mill, which will extract the seeds as it purees. (Removing the seeds is optional but would have been done in houses like Downton.) Combine the cream and superfine

sugar in a bowl, and using a whisk or a handheld mixer on medium speed, whip together until soft peaks form. Gently fold in the raspberry puree just until no white streaks remain. Taste and adjust with confectioners' sugar if you prefer it sweeter. The fool should be fairly tart, however, to contrast with the meringue.
5. Both the meringues and the fool can be made a day in advance. Store the meringues in an airtight container at room temperature and the fool tightly covered in the fridge. When you are ready to serve, fill the meringue nests with the fool, and top with the small meringues. Serve with raspberries alongside.

AUTHOR'S NOTE If it goes a bit wrong and the meringue nests break or don't harden evenly, simply break them up roughly and mix them with the whipped

cream, the raspberry puree and a few whole raspberries and call it a Downton mess (if you use strawberries, it's the classic Eton mess, named for the school to which most aristocratic boys were sent at the time). You can replace the raspberries with strawberries, blackberries, blueberries, gooseberries or plums (the latter two need to be simmered with a little water to soften before you puree them). The fool is also good on its own, served in glasses on a summer day.

From *The Official Downton Abbey Cookbook* written by Annie Gray, published by Weldon Owen © 2019 by Carnival Films & Television Ltd

CREDITS

A NEW ERA
All photos: Ben Blackall/© 2021 Focus
Features, LLC

PROFILES OF THE STARS
28-29 Jaap Buitendijk/© 2019 Focus Features,
LLC; **31** D Dipasupil/FilmMagic/Getty Images;
34 Magnus Sundholm/Shutterstock;
35 (Pamuk) Focus Features; **39** David M.
Benett/Getty Images; **43** (Gregson) David
M. Benett/Getty Images; (Bertie) Focus
Features; **45** Alamy; **47** (Leech) Gregory
Pace/Shutterstock; **48** Ben Blackall/© 2022
Focus Features LLC; **49** Gregory Pace/
Shutterstock; **50** Shutterstock; **53** Joan
Wakeham/Shutterstock; **54** Anthony Harvey/
Shutterstock; **55** Giles Keyte/Carnival Film &
Television Limited; **58** (Ethel) Focus Features;
(Spratt) Photofest; (Denker) MWE/GC
Images/Getty Images; **59** (Rosamund) Focus
Features; **60** Shutterstock; All other photos:
Nick Briggs/Carnival Film & Television Limited

MUST-SEE MOMENTS
68 Everett Collection; All other photos: Nick
Briggs/Carnival Film & Television Limited

DOWNTON & HISTORY
70 (clockwise from top left) The Print
Collector/Getty Images; Bettmann/Getty
Images; Everett Collection; Nick Briggs/
Carnival Film & Television Limited(2);
71 (clockwise from top) Carnival Film &
Television Limited 2011; LMPC/Getty Images;
Buyenlarge/Getty Images; Bettmann/Getty
Images; Alamy

IN THEIR OWN WORDS
72-73 Jaap Buitendijk/© 2019 Focus Features,
LLC; **74-75** Jaap Buitendijk/© 2019 Focus
Features, LLC; **76** Carnival Film & Television
Limited; **77** Alamy; **78** Nick Briggs/The
New York Times/Redux; **79-80** Nick Briggs/
Carnival Film & Television Limited(3); **81** Ben
Blackall/© 2022 Focus Features LLC

DRESSING *DOWNTON*
82-83 Liam Daniel/© 2019 Focus Features;
84, 86 Jaap Buitendijk/© 2019 Focus
Features, LLC; All other photos: Nick Briggs/
Carnival Film & Television Limited

INSIDE HIGHCLERE CASTLE
88 Rex/Rex USA/Shutterstock; **89-90** Ilpo
Musto/Shutterstock(3); **90** (lower left) Nick
Briggs/Carnival Film & Television Limited
2012; **91** (top) Rex/Rex USA/Shutterstock(2);
(bottom) Carnival Film & Television Limited

SPECIALTIES OF THE HOUSE
92 Carnival Film & Television Limited 2012;
93 Nick Briggs/Carnival Film & Television
Limited; **94** From The Official Downton Abbey
Cookbook © Carnival Film & Television Ltd
published by Weldon Owen.
Photo by John Kernick

DID YOU KNOW?
96 Nick Briggs/Carnival Film & Television
Limited 2015

BACK COVER
Ben Blackall/© 2021 Focus Features, LLC

FRONT COVER
Jason Bell/©2022 Focus Features LLC

TITLE PAGE/ TOC
1 istock/Getty Images; **2-3** Alamy

INTRO
4-5 Jaap Buitendijk / Focus Features

A STELLAR ENSEMBLE
6-7 Nick Briggs/Carnival Film
& Television Limited

PEOPLE
President Leah Wyar
Editor Liz Vaccariello
Creative Director Andrea Dunham
Director of Photography
Ilana Schweber
Director of Editorial Operations
Alexandra Brez

PEOPLE BOOKS
Editor Allison Adato
Edition Editor Richard Jerome
Art Director Greg Monfries
Photo Editor C.Tiffany Lee
Deputy Art Director Lisa Kelsey
Contributing Photo Editor
Louis Pearlman
Writers Rebecca Ascher-Walsh,
Bill Keith
Reporters Gillian Aldrich, Stewart Allen,
Mary Hart
Copy Desk Joanann Scali (Chief),
James Bradley (Deputy), Ellen Adamson,
Gabrielle Danchick, Rich Donnelly,
Shakthi Jothianandan, Matt Weingarden
(Copy Editors)
Production Designers Peter Niceberg,
Lori Cervone
Premedia Trafficking Supervisor
Greg Fairholm
Premedia Imaging Specialist
Don Atkinson
Color Quality Analysts
Rob Roszkowski, Sara Luckey

PEOPLE Public Relations Julie Farin,
Marnie Perez

DOTDASH MEREDITH
PREMIUM PUBLISHING
Vice President & General Manager
Jeremy Biloon
Vice President, Group Editorial Director
Stephen Orr
Director, Brand Marketing
Jean Kennedy
Associate Director, Brand Marketing
Bryan Christian
Senior Brand Manager
Katherine Barnet

Editorial Director Kostya Kennedy
Creative Director Gary Stewart
Director of Photography
Christina Lieberman
Editorial Operations Director
Jamie Roth Major
Manager, Editorial Operations
Gina Scauzillo

Special Thanks Brad Beatson, Samantha
Lebofsky, Kate Roncinske, Céline Wojtala

DIGITAL
President Leah Wyar
VP/Group General Manager, People
Zoe Ruderman

Gillian Anderson was originally offered the part of Cora.

Alastair Bruce, *Downton Abbey*'s historical adviser, made a cameo in each season.

Laura Carmichael (Lady Edith) kept a folder on her phone of GIFs to make Maggie Smith laugh, titled "pictures for Maggie." Smith was especially fond of ones featuring cats.

Harry Hadden-Paton, who plays Herbert Pelham, is the godson of Sarah Ferguson, the Duchess of York.

There was only one bedroom set for Edith, Mary and Cora—it was redecorated for each character.

Elizabeth McGovern (Countess Cora) has a folk-rock band called Sadie and the Hotheads.

DID YOU KNOW?

EVEN DEVOTED DOWNTONISTAS MAY NOT BE FAMILIAR WITH THESE FUN FACTS

Made in United States
Orlando, FL
02 June 2022

18427984R00055